T0374086

INSIDE THE MUSE

by Thomas MacCalla

Copyright 2017 by Thomas A. MacCalla, All rights reserved

Kin Pro Communications, LLC, Del Mar, California
Publishing@Kinpro-communications.com
&
XLIBRIS LLC, Bloomberg, Indiana
www.Xlibris.com

No part of this multimedia publication may be reproduced, stored in a retrieval system, or transmitted, in any form
or by any means, without the prior permission in writing from the publisher or as expressly permitted by law.

Library of Congress Cataloging-in-Publication Data available

ISBN: Softcover   978-1-5245-7006-4
        EBook   978-1-5245-7007-1

Cover Design by John Walker
Photographs, music, and artworks by Thomas MacCalla,
Reuben MacCalla, Sylvia Moore, and Courtesy Contributors

Print information available on the last page

Rev. date: 05/02/2017

To order additional copies of this book, contact:
Xlibris
1-888-795-4274
www.Xlibris.com
Orders@Xlibris.com

TABLE OF CONTENTS

DEDICATION

To Jacqueline Caesar MacCalla and our grandchildren
Evan Masterman, Ande Jay and Sebastian MacCalla, Ben and
Jim Niedzialkowski, and David Loreke

Preface

INSIDE THE MUSE is a sequel to *Artistry in Word Music* (2014) and a showcasing of visual verse and companion imagery called "Poetraitures." Visit the exhibit halls of the poetic artifcats that hang on the hooks of the mind and enjoy the virtual tour.

INSIDE THE MUSE

Poetry mixes thoughts and emotions,
and blends them with imagination's chords
to produce songs of the human spirit
expressing the essence of one's being.

Experience the word music artifacts
on display inside the museum-like
and enjoy the virtual tour
of muse murals on display.

Framing the Poetraitures

Poetraitures is a collection of multimedia poetry and prose that visualizes what the mind sees, the heart feels, and imagination creates. It is a sequel to the earlier *Artistry in Word Music* (2014), which was a collage of verse and visuals echoing thoughts and emotions of the human spirit. The collection shares the observations and concerns of an octogenarian, who invites the reader-viewer to go on a virtual tour Inside the Muse.

The tour begins with a display of Muse Murals introduced by a "welcome to Del Mar" and is followed by a panorama of Nature's beauty in the open and glances at daily life. The next showing is a montage of cultural impressions and expressions ending with a plea for greater awareness of the looming environmental threat called the Anthropocence.

The muse walk continues with a set of cameos on learning, our knowledge quest, fantasy, and nostalgia. The reflective mood then shifts to an exploration of the Mindsphere and the Planet of the Mind with a commentary on consciousness and possibility of a cosmic connection. The virtual visit ends with a script about the author and his passion for poetry.

Part 1: Muse Murals

Muse Murals are portraiture exhibits that hang on the curiosity hooks of the mind. The first depicts the instant of the Now and its lasting presence. The others display features of Nature's beauty in the open and glimpse at phases in our life span.

FOREVER NOW

Now is an awareness of the moment
fusing past present with present future
that is indelibly inscribed in the mind
to experience a fleeting instant
as a presence lingering forever.

WELCOME TO DEL MAR

Welcome to Del Mar's early evening show
where Nature's poetry is on display
with the rising and setting of the sun
before the stars parade in the night sky.

Sense the swaying of beauty in the open,
where azure blue waters shape the stanzas
with shoreline vistas and etchings of earth
staring at the expanse in silence.

BEYOND THE BLUE

*See the panoramic Pacific view
of boundless sky and water wilderness
as a portrait of an open window
to the infinite realm Beyond the Blue.*

POETRY OF THE OUTDOORS

See the recurring ritual of dusk
produce a poem of natural beauty
with hovering clouds forming a night shade
drawn to darkness until the dawn returns

Enjoy the imagery of evening calm
posing in the warmth of a summer breeze
to portray the artisty of Nature
as poetry written without words.

NEWNESS

Behold the radiant image of spring
reflecting the ritual of newness
and invigorating the sense of hope
with its gracefulness and silent beauty.

A SILENT SONG

Instantly today becomes tomorrow,
echoing the silence of the moment
in the chamber of the now that we own.

Imagination bridges the unseen
and allows us to fathom forever
despite the limits of logic and faith.

As we continue to search for meaning
and await the everlasting promise,
we are plagued with uncertainty and doubt.

In the meantime enjoy love and freedom
savoring memories of yesteryears
and pursuing the dreams we put on hold.

Praise the innocence in eyes of children,
aware of how time will steal it away
so they can discover truth on their own.

Listen to the tune of integrity
where we are true to ourselves and others,
and our belief systems find common ground.

FLOWER FEELS

See the delicate array of flowers
colorfully gathered in the open
celebrating the miracle of life
with their sunlit smiles of vitality.

Bask in the warmth of the Oloral landscape
greeting onlookers with welcoming smiles
recollecting the artistry created
by the font of life and source of beauty.

LOOK OF LIFE

A seasoned face reveals a life's journey
through experienced eyes and a sage smile
personifying pride, love and kindness
beyond the blur of hurt and sacrifice.

AGING

Aging is being aware of spent time
and having to listen to the body
trying to adjust and accommodate
the annoying feeling of wear and tear.

Recalling the past and looking ahead,
coupled with the need to keep love alive
as the faint sound of footsteps grow louder,
becomes a quiet preoccupation.

Override those thought out of your control
by enjoying the gift of another day,
celebrating the joy of the moment
and appreciating relationships.

LATER YEARS

When we hear footsteps in our later years
we become more conscious of fleeting time,
wanting to reminisce and asking questions
about the choices made and where they led,

We're curious about uncertainty,
and the chasing sound of finality
focusing on the treasure of today
rather than the promise of tomorrow.

Before we cross the finish line speak out
to those admired and depend on us
about accepting the life as they find it
and caring, love, and forgiveness

Strive to live a life of integrity,
making adjustments dictated by age,
encouraging others to keep the faith,
and enjoy the beauty of the moment.

LOVE VIEW

Love is a personal relationship,
a mutual bond of commitment
to caring, sacrifice, and forgiveness
forged by honest hearts united as one
and reflecting the Everlasting Light.

Part 2 - Cultural Impressions

Cultural impressions characterize expressions of humanity's historical record and descriptors of people associated with national origin, ethnicity and racial identity. They also project cross-patterns of behavior prone to generalizations. The cultural markers in this section are imprints of a global whole and imply an inherent desire to seek knowledge and improve the quality of life.

CULTURE

*Stories, symbols, rituals, and legends
are recognizable traits of culture
associated with people and place
expressing beliefs, belonging, and pride
and leaving memorable impressions*

WE

*Who are the people referred to as Them
and why are They so different from Us
because when together, they become We.*

GLOBAL WEAVE

Touch the tapestry of global culture
and iconic images symbolizing
people, places, and historical pasts.

See hues of diversity and freedom
with variations on democracy
and respect for life and equality.

Sense the universal nature of love
on a canvas of concern and caring
coated with openness and forgiveness.

Feel the fabric of cultural oneness,
woven with threads of interdependence
inclusiveness, prosperity, and peace.

FLAGS OF THE ROUND

Flags of the Round symbolize globalism
circling our interdependent world
with national markers of diversity.

America's flag flies opportunity
waving the striped banner of democracy
with colors of freedom and justice for all.

Other furled signatures of collective pride
reflect the hues of cultural differences
with variations on rights and governance.

Appreciate the flag of togetherness
flying over the human community
sharing global knowledge, love, and compassion.

MAYBE

Worrisome winds of the impersonal
and threatening clouds of indifference
should make us rethink our view of the world.

Can we appreciate differences
in people, cultures, customs, and beliefs
and accept the consequences of change?

Can we start questioning our assumptions
about absolutes and doubtful dictates
and collaborate on solving problems?

Maybe we should recalibrate our visions
with commitments to mutual respect,
openness, knowledge sharing, and global trust.

Maybe we could create a communal world
that reaches beyond national borders
and breeds respect for human dignity.

WONDER LANDS

Costa Rica, a country of contrasts,
inland empire of pristine beauty
with volcanoes, rain forests, and beaches ,
exotic birds, butterflies and gardens,
complementing the cultural warmth
and diversity of its populous.

Croatia, the wonder land of Europe
and heritage site of antiquity,
crowned with a jewel of cascading waterfalls
and thousands of lakes set in greenery
fronted by a spectacular coastline
as a natural tribute to beauty.

Courtesy of Donna Masterman

Cross-Cultural Plea: The Anthropocene

Sustaining the life of the planet is everyone's responsibility, one that crosses cultures and boundaries. The plea offered here addresses a looming threat of global devastation referred to as the Anthropocene, the next geological time period or epoch.

Even though the evidence of humanity's influence and disastrous impact on the Earth's atmospheric, geologic, and biospheric systems is compelling, all is not lost. We still have a chance to avoid the doomsday forecasts if we are more aware and collectively ready to make a serious effort to change our detrimental patterns of behavior.

First of all, we must recognize our vulnerability, the issues that contribute to the problem, and our capacity to change direction for the better. We need to generate widespread awareness of the possible consequences and engage people locally and globally so that they can alter detrimental patterns of behavior.

The choice is ours. As planetary futurist Alex Steffen poignantly stated, "The sustainability we face now is not a matter of taking things we already do and make them a little less bad, but rather doing new things."

OUR CHOICE

*Who are the dwellers sharing the planet
unaware of their interdependence
and the consequences of their actions?*

*We all should care about the biosphere
since what we do today shapes tomorrow
and have a chance to make a difference.*

*Counter the threat of the Anthropocene
or accept the forecast of the pending doom
looming over the survival of earth.*

Let us take responsibility
for charting a new course of destiny
and seed hope for generations to come.

Hands of humanity circle the globe
symbolizing the protection of Earth
against the threat of man-made disaster.

We are the agents of planet change,
contributors to the Anthropocence
and the best source for our own salvation.

Let's take local and global action
to foster an awareness of the forces
depleting finite natural resources.

Harness the energy of everyone
to curb pollution and population,
combat poverty and exploitation.

Engage people in revitalizing
our environs and use technology
to facilitate and compensate.

NATURAL BALANCE

What if we set imagination free
to visualize the impossible
and create ideas that tease the mind
with the wisdom found in simplicity,

Can we envision another world
where everyone shares the others' burden
and inclusiveness with social justice
becomes the universal rule of law.

Can we commit, on every level
to saving and sustaining the planet,
by changing our consumption behavior
and be more aware of Nature's needs.

Recognize the strength of diversity
and commonality in differences,
including agreeing to disagree
and diplomacy to counteract war.

The secret is a natural balance
on a life scale of love and compassion
that exemplifies our togetherness
and ensures a sustainable future.

Part 3: Cameos

Cameos are observations and commentary on the ordinary and the imaginary. They begin with an invitation to journey on the open road without a destination. Along the way, insights on mind matters and life lessons appear and fade away. The experience ends on a fantasy note with virtual wine tasting and a rekindling of a musical era with picturesque jazz and a melodic portrait called Dream In Blue.

OPEN ROAD

*Journey freely without a destination
to experience the joy of wanderlust
and start living dreams that were put on hold.*

LIVE AND LEARN

We live to learn and learn to live not knowing why,
defining ourselves despite what others may think,
willing to share what we know and help when we can
and contribute to the greater good.

Discover the secret to living and learning
and the treasure vault of an open mind and heart
search for the door to knowledge and the key to love
and honor the gift of life and pursuit of peace.

KNOWLEDGE QUEST

Creativity is birthing newness,
skirting the edge of the impossible
with the power of imagination
to satisfy curiosity's urge
and release the spirit of uniqueness.

Innovation is finding solutions
to seemingly insolvable problems
and discovering ways to unravel
mysteries with novel ideas
that stimulate and create something new.

Collaboration is togetherness,
the sum of we as one to solve problems
with innovation, creativity
and inclusive involvement of people
with a shared mission for the common good.

LIGHT OF DATA

Learning starts where we are and never ends,
turning information into knowledge
and transforming insights into wisdom
that advances mankind and new knowledge.

The light of data shines on the unseen
visualizing the depths of detail
for greater insight on the probable
and implications for the possible.

TECHNOLOGY

Technology is a powerful tool
that can improve the quality of life
or be used to divide and conquer.

Since we are the designers and builders
of this masterful mechanical mind,
we must ensure the good and thwart the bad.

Technology should enhance human work
and enable us to shape a future
that advances humanity's progress.

Appreciate technology's treasures
and the knowledge advantage that it spawns
while empowering those in greatest need.

Increase awareness and education
and tap the potential of everyone,
foster innovation and promote peace.

Utilize collective intelligence
across generation, cultures and place
to optimize our interdependence.

HONEST DOUBT

Curiosity is a source of doubt,
and the engine of creativity,
questioning the truth of everything
in search of new paths to discovery..

Honest doubt is inherently wise,
removing obscurity from view
opening windows to transparency
for the free flow of objectivity.

EMPOWERMENT

Curiosity breeds discovery,
questioning everything to know more
and nurtures seeds of imagination
to create alternative ways of thinking.

The constant of change and uncertainty
enable us to adjust to newness
and capitalize on the knowledge gained
to better understand complexity.

Pursue the awesome of power knowledge
and use its power for the greater good
by sharing its strength with the least informed.
and advancing the cause of humanity.

PARENTHOOD

Parents raise children who become parents
and grow to know each other over time
as guardians, givers, and life-long friends.

They nurture the importance of self worth,
encouraging offspring to be themselves
and become the best person they can be.

Parents recognize the flight of youth
and accept the avalanche of aging
with the hope of leaving a legacy.

They instill pride, responsibility,
and sense of family togetherness,
caring and sharing themselves with others.

REALITY CHECK

Preparing children for the inevitable
is a difficult and delicate matter
that needs to be conveyed and understand
so they can deal with loss and carry on.

Age deterioration is a concern
that can also rival the pain of grief
and calls upon parents to address it
with a reality conversion.

Mothers and fathers are the pillars
of love, strength, wisdom and encouragement,
perceived as the font of family knowledge
and enablers of a better life.

Offspring are the beneficiaries
of bounty beyond the material
and sibling contributors to caring
recognizing the gift of love received.

Hopefully, wellness decisions are shared
and accepted by the children involved
with an assumption of obligations
and honoring the will of the parents.

When the final curtain is drawing near
the overarching sentiment is thanks
and the wholesome spirit of family
with the sharing of love with one another.

GENERATION OF THE FUTURE

Children and grandchildren are our future
so we should make an investment in them
through mutual exchange of ideas
positive thinking, and good examples.

The future is constantly emerging
and shaped inter-generationally
by valuing what is deemed important,
and working toward a change for the better.

Perspectives on what we value the most
differ among people in time and place,
conditioned by prevailing social norms
and the assumptions preserving the past.

May the generation of the future
preserve our freedoms and pursue greatness
for themselves, their children, and grandchildren
as the next champions of tomorrow..

FRACTURED FUTURE

The future is constructing tomorrow
with shared concerns and sense of unity
amidst uncertainty and constant change.

As we look through today's murky mirror,
we see rising fear and divisiveness
mounting an attack on civility.

Public concern over terrorism
and uneasiness with law enforcement
suggest a future that could be fractured.

Together we can end the violence,
champion the right of peaceful protest,
the rule of law and those who protect it.

We have come a long way in righting wrongs
but we must keep building mutual trust
and respecting differences in the world.

The future should reflect the best of We,
appreciating diversity's strength
and sharing our resources with others.

Envision a community of wholeness
with a culture of collaboration
trust, equality and inclusiveness.

Foster the importance of We as One
and value of global citizenship
to keep the emerging future intact.

DOG TALK

Talks with my friend Jake on our daily walks
offer insights on how dogs think and feel,
and a sense of their intuitiveness.

Apart from conditioned obedience,
dogs are driven by a mind of their own
eager to run, play, eat, and mark their spot.

Dogs talk with their eyes, readily reply,
and stare with affection for attention,
hoping for approval and a reward.

Dogs have a keen sense of sounds and voices
anticipate behaviors and commands
and demonstrate they understand words..

Engage in dog talk on your next dog walk
to gain more insight on their expression
and notice how much we have in common.

RE-RUN

Awoke to the dawning of a new day
and gratefully gave thanks for being alive.

Thought about the dream ride in slumber land
and wondered about its breadth of meaning.

Recalled running along memory lane
with the feeling of yesterday in tow.

Mixed random fragments from the days before
so the impossible was possible.

Retrieved fantasies freely on display
to become invincible and insightful.

Ascended to a higher state of mind,
to know more about life and meaning.

I yearned to know the other side of doubt.
and felt the horizon of hope was near.

Spoke to familiar folks who once were
and talked with them as though they did not leave.

Hopefully tomorrow will greet me again
and the wonder of my dreams will return.

VIRTUAL WINE TASTING

Enjoy fermented grapes from my vineyard
cultivated in a fantasy world
visible to closed eyes with open minds

Hold the half-filled crystal, ready to salute
with a make-believe swirl of the liquid
in anticipation of approval.

Now join me in a simulated toast
with a mindful sip of virtual wine
on the occasion of our shared interests.

Recreate a Pinot Noir sensation
with a thought taste of cyber nectar
pleasing the palate with a hint of fruit.

Now relax in the comfort of knowing
you can enjoy imaginary wine
and share the virtual experience.

PICTURESQUE JAZZ

Rekindle the spirit of a jazz era
when one could hear "Knock on Wood" at the Lighthouse
or the sounds of bee bop from Gillespie's horn
punctuated with "Salt Peanuts, Salt Peanuts."

Reminisce with Sassy Sarah's add-lib runs
and Lady Ella's phrasign with dulcet tones
or George Shearing's "I Only Have Eyes for You."
with distinctive block chords crossing the ocean.

Revisit Kenton's "Artistry in Rhythm,"
Sauter and Finegan's swing jazz orchestra,
the Count and Duke, or Goodman and the Dorseyes
exemplifying the best of the big bands.

Savor these sounds with the joy of nostalgia
and the funk of Miles, Monks, and Montgomery
passed on to youth talents to carry the torch
as jazz aficionados in their winter years.

MUSICAL PORTRAIT

Dream in Blue

You blew into my life like the wind
A love so strong don't know where I begin
When suddenly you left without a sound
I sit in pieces just waiting to be found
I can't even lay my head upon the pillow to dream
cause when I do I dream in blue I dream blue

Once unafraid to love I pulled you in
tempted by your touch almost like a sin
Never realizing you might slip away
I'm just a shell of all my yesterday's
I can't even lay my head upon the pillow to dream
cause when I do I dream in blue I dream of blue.

Part 4 - Exploring the Mindsphere

Welcome to the Mindsphere and the Planet of the Mind, and join me on a virtual voyage through inner and outer spaces probing the nature of consciousness and its cosmic connection. The trek also envisions possible access to the Akasha, the purported library of all events and responses concerning consciousness from the beginning of space-time.

The mind is the source of consciousness, determiner of reality and reflector of the human spirit Even though theologians and philosophers consider the concept of consciousness to be inherently unknowable, scientist continue to pursue an understanding its nature and develop a testable scientific theory for its existence and function.

Rene Descartes 17th century proclamation "cogito ergo sum" or "I Think, therefore I am" was an early attempt to identify the" mind at work." Current descriptions of consciousness see it as the "awareness of being aware" or "the state of being awake and aware of what is happening around you, and of having a sense of self? The mind is associated with the brain and is also considered a non-physical entity or the font of human spirit.

Present-day Neuroscientists seek to discover specific neurons or behaviors that are linked to conscious experiences and have developed theories to advance the cause. Most notable are 1) Integrated Information, which explains how the brain produces subjective experiences, and 2) Global Workplace, or a computerized memory bank.

"Exploring the Mindsphere" is an explanation of the phenomenon that ventures into an imaginary world of possibilities. It also considers energy as the all-encompassing fabric of the universe. Consciousness makes it real.

CONSCIOUSNESS

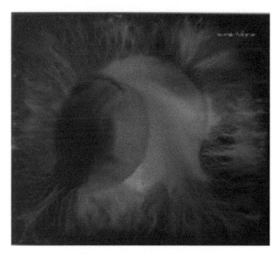

*Consciousness is the essence of being,
creator of our own realities,
perceived, experienced, and imagined,
mirroring the mind and human spirit
embedded in eternal energy.*

PLANET OF THE MIND

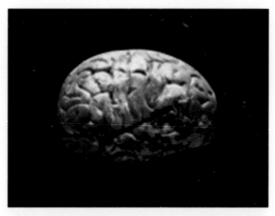

The Planet of the Mind is a thought space
connected to a cosmic consciousness
of an intelligent unified field
embedded in a limitless universe.

Explore this inner domain of the self
through introspection and speculation
and stream invisible energy waves
with a heightened sense of consciousness.

Search for clues to a cosmic connection
and align thought vibration frequencies
with the wave lengths of information stored
in the Akashic Record forever.

Consider the possibility of
knowing more with limited knowledge
and contributing to the greater good
as an inherent human quality.

STAR STUFF

We are flashes of life made of star stuff,
continually evolving creatures
on an evolutionary spiral
of human growth and development
attesting to mankind's finite existence
in the spiritual realm of a cosmos
created from nothing with lasting love.

COSMIC CONNECTION

A powerful light of eternal love
sparked a singularity implosion
that created perpetual energy
with a big bang spewing the stuff of stars
in a conscious and expanding cosmos.

FATHOMING THE UNKNOWN

We are curious about the unknown,
the source of life, the font of existence,
and the prospect of living afterward.

Come with me on a virtual voyage
and explore the expanse of the unknown
with the power of imagination.

Let the seemingly inconceivable
surface and consume your every thought
and envision roaming in the new space.

Listen to the silence of your spirit
plea for belief in the unknowable
with the echoes of logic's resistance.

Explore the deep labyrinth of the mind
and converse with the other you inside
to override doubt and discover Truth.

Ascending to a higher state of mind
makes fathoming the unknown possible,
especially if you believe in you.

WHEREVER YOU ARE

Where are the loved ones and dear companions
now peacefully at rest in memories,
reminding us of fond relationships
and commitments that covered a lifetime?

Can we skirt the edge of wishful thinking
and reestablish communications
through the thought waves of the human spirit
steeped in the perpetual energy field?

Follow the footsteps of the soulful self
that lead to the open door of dream space,
renewing the joy of togetherness
and the sharing of pleasurable thoughts.

By consciously aligning frequencies
in the unified field of the cosmos
we may be able to sense your presence
and orbit the eternal Light of Love.

STAYING ALIVE

We live as long as those who knew us were here
and our spiritual presence is kept alive
through joyful memories of togetherness.

Those left behind await their final call
and acknowledge the life of those who once were
while hoping that they too will be remembered.

What if we could flee the illusion of time
and ride invisible waves of energy
to quell the chasing sound of finality.

What if we used imagination's power
to envision tomorrow through the mind's eye
and recreated the impossible dream.

What if we knew the mysterious unknown
and basked in the sun of a boundless beyond
waiting for the voice of perpetual peace.

May the wishful thought of eternal peace
erase hovering fears of dead and gone
to stay alive in the minds of others.

ABOUT THE AUTHOR

Life Lines:

Thomas A. MacCalla, or TAM, is an educator and self-styled poet. He was born in Bridgeport, Connecticut in 1929 and started his poetry dream ride in 1998 with the publication of Sepiatones. The ride continued with Rhythm & Musein 2007, Artistry in Word Music in 2014, and now with a 2017 guided tour Inside the Muse.

TAM was educated by the Jesuits at Fairfield University in Connecticut. He graduated from Fairfield College Preparatory School in 1947 and received both bachelors and masters degrees from Fairfield University in the 1950s. He later attended the University of California, Los Angeles, where he earned his doctorate and pursued post-doctoral studies.

TAM was a high school teacher, assistant school district superintendent, a college professor, and a vice president at National University in San Diego, California. He also was a former Marine Corps Officer and Korean War Vet who served as a Platoon Commander and Division Historical Officer.

PASSION FOR POETRY

Playing with words to visualize thought
and conceptualize fantasy
fuels my passion for writing poetry.

The mental montage becomes word music
produced and performed on a digital stage
as muse murals reflecting my world view.

Behind the seen are measured syllables
that keep the verbal images moving
enhancing the flow of the sentiment.

Printed in the United States
By Bookmasters